THE PAIN

A BLACK MAN'S POETIC REFLECTIONS ON EMOTIONAL PAIN & MENTAL DISTRESS

THE PAIN
A Black Man's Poetic Reflections on
Emotional Pain & Mental Distress

Copyright © 2021 Michael Simmons

All scripture references used in this book were taken from the Holy Bible, New International Version and can be found at http://thebiblegateway.com.

ISBN: 978-1-7365129-2-0

10 9 8 7 6 5 4 3 2 1
Printed in the United States

Priceless Publishing
Coral Springs, Fl www.pricelesspublishing.co

CONTENTS.

PART I.

PART II.

INTRO.

Sitting in a dark bedroom with just a night lamp, listening to the combined sounds of thunderstorms and jazz music, I write this book. I know that this comes during an unfortunate and unprecedented time in the world where we all — regardless of age, race, sex or faith — are experiencing some amount of growing pain from adjusting and adapting to new normals.

As you can tell by the title of the book, I don't write to you from a place of happiness. Instead, I write from a place of awareness, — that only I can control how I feel, and triumph, — that I have exited a very dark and seemingly endless tunnel of mental health challenges.

This book isn't about physical pain — it's about mental pain. For anyone who is now, or has ever been uncomfortable talking about their own painful mental health issues, read on.

My objective at the end of this book is to create an authentic visualization of a picture made by my words. All poems included are originals. I hope you and I end up relating to each other on some level throughout this reading journey. Consider this a therapy session for realizing, unleashing and embracing your pain.

MICHAEL

PART I.

BEFORE THE PAIN

WHO AM I?

Before I talk about my pain, let me tell you a little about myself. I'm Michael Simmons and I have suffered from mental health issues — specifically anxiety and depression. Growing up, I seldom expressed my feelings as I observed and was taught that doing so would paint me as weak — and weakness in a black man is frowned upon.

WEAK OR JUST HUMAN?

Weakness, as it was taught to me, is a detriment, a disease, a smear on your identity as a black man. Furthermore, to be a black man verbalizing mental health challenges is even more laughable and unaccepted. The taught ideal was for me to *grin and bear it* while simultaneously pretending that my challenges were non-existent.

But as I got older and despite all the opposition, I started to get comfortable expressing how I truly feel. Suffering in silence and feigning wellness had proven to be ineffective strategies. So, I got involved in athletics.

However, playing sports exacerbated my mental health issues. The constant and heavy pressure put on you to succeed in athletics can fuel insecurities and fears of inadequacy. My internal dialogue would sound like this:

Am I good enough?

Can I do it?

They are all expecting me to fail anyways.

Do I really love this?

MY DISGUISED IDENTITY

He hides within himself from self-reflection.

Buried beneath all the praise, success and applause of others is a constant and unrelenting voice of sabotage.

Ego keeps him high above all the rest.

He is puffed up.

Unreachable from those who truly care.

*Ego keeps him out of the grasp of reality
Placing him in the hands of fantasy's snare.*

*Ego shouts out in foreign voice that
he isn't good enough.*

Ego turns his joy into self-doubt.

Ego will ruin his life.

- EGO

That's the pain I hide. I try not to let the bad days define me. But my ego is something I use to mask the insecurities I have within myself. I make people feel what I feel sometimes simply because it seems people won't accept the real me.

I'm the kid who everyone thinks has it all together but doesn't know what he's doing with this life he's been given. Makes me sound aloof and ungrateful, right? *Like what kind of person/man could be so self-absorbed that he doesn't see how good he has it?*

They were all wrong. I was just a kid who wanted someone to talk to but just couldn't seem to find a consistent listener. I often ask myself why do we feel this way or why do I feel this way. I pray to GOD and ask him to take these unfamiliar sensitivities away from me.

TO ME, PAIN IS LIKE LIFTING WEIGHTS IN ORDER TO GET STRONGER — YOU HAVE TO FEEL IT.

In response, it's seems like GOD says, "When you're at your weakest is when I can help you the most". 2 Corinthians 12:9 NIV reminds me of this and it has since become one of my favorite scriptures.

"BUT HE SAID TO ME, "MY GRACE IS SUFFICIENT FOR YOU, FOR MY POWER IS MADE PERFECT IN WEAKNESS." THEREFORE I WILL BOAST ALL THE MORE GLADLY ABOUT MY WEAKNESSES, SO THAT CHRIST'S POWER MAY REST ON ME."

Here's a word of encouragement to you: the weakest point in your life can be your strongest based on what you do in that state.

LET ME TELL YOU WHAT MY PAIN REALLY IS.

My pain is being the person everyone comes to when they feel loss and discomfort in this world. My pain is being everyone's therapist but not having therapy of my own.

When I listen to people's problems, I occasionally close my eyes and wonder to myself, *"Do they know that my phone number is the same when they are happy?"* They won't even bother picking up the phone to contact me when everything is good with them. If the roles were reversed and I needed to vent, I know their time would be limited.

As if we don't have the same 24 hours every day.

I feel unwanted yet needed, kinda like when you're sick, you don't want to get a shot but you know you need it in order to get better. That's what I detect people think of me - a necessary pain. I'm starting to find a simple way to clarify my pain.

I FEEL USED.

LOVING SOMEBODY WHO DOESN'T LOVE BACK

I see you as more than just a body.

*I don't feel like there is a specific
criteria for beauty.*

*But if I had to define beauty,
the example would be you.*

*You don't have to degrade yourself for a man seeking
an ego boost, just so you can feel worthy enough.*

*By existing you are worthy of love.
I love all the things about you.*

*I love your hair, so curly and thick.
I love your eyes, so brown and wide.
I love their gleam when you look into mine.*

*If I could give you one thing in life,
I'd give you the power to see yourself through my eyes.*

*Only then, possibly, would you realize
how special you are to me.*

- BEAUTIFUL BLACK GIRL

To me, love is strange. There is never really any satisfaction in it. It's a drug that I got so addicted to once, that it led to heartbreak.

SHE WAS SO BEAUTIFUL.
SO BEAUTIFUL THAT I DEFINED HER AS BEAUTY.

The fact that I thought someone like her actually loved me. Place after place, date after date...it's like we were caught up in a whirlwind. It got to the point where no sooner would one date finish than I would get a text with the next place that we will visit. It was always a place that we have never been to before. We were creating new experiences.

What an amazing month that was. It felt like a movie. Only a day would pass and it felt like I hadn't seen her in weeks. There was just so much to talk about! It was almost as if time was not enough to contain all that we had to share. Every day I thought to myself, *"Today's the day. I'm going to tell her how I really feel about her."*

BUT IN THE BLINK OF AN EYE, THINGS CHANGED.

"He texted me," she said, speaking of her ex.

This ex was a guy who had already broken her heart once before. I felt as if her heart was a broken toy that I had mended, just to have it snatched away by the person who broke it. I can't put into words how insecure and unworthy I felt in that moment. One thing was certain: this attempt at opening up my heart to someone has failed.

It feels like I'm taking a test that is impossible to pass. Not just any test, it's like an essay exam paper that you didn't study for. There are not even any multiple-choice options to give you a hint so you can pass. I was only temporarily cherished. I told myself I won't feel this feeling ever again.

I politely declined the next outing request with a text of my own.

"We can't hangout anymore".

I guess we don't always get the fairy tale ending, do we?

LOVE.

I tell myself I'll never love anyone ever again. But even while I say it, I know that it is a lie. I'm starting to get better at just going with the flow and not letting someone manipulate or control my emotions — or at least I am trying. Loving someone who doesn't love you back can feel unbearable but we just have to deal with it.

I FEEL UNLOVED.

ISOLATED CONTEMPLATION

"Have you ever lost someone you loved?

Have you ever thought the time you spent away from them is the reason they are gone?

Have you ever sat and cried filled with regret That while alive you didn't cherish them?

Have you ever looked in the mirror and had a vision?

That seemed like an optical illusion, That you don't want to wake up from.

Have you ever listened to a certain song and heard their voice?

Because I have."

- HAVE YOU EVER

The reduced ability to concentrate, make decisions, problem solve, and even change negative self-talk — this is the epitome of loneliness. For me, it was a period characterized by endless tears and a lot of confusion. Confusion as to why GOD didn't answer my prayer to save her.

"I CAN'T BREATHE."

Those were the words of my 8 year old sister, as she experienced what would be, her last asthma attack. Those were words that I had heard from her before but this time felt different in a way I couldn't possibly articulate. I was only 12 years old and at the time, I don't think I had fully grasped the gravity of the situation. I only know that I felt fear and worry, as my Dad rushed her to the hospital.

When I woke up the next morning, no announcement was needed. I could just feel it. She was gone. I was broken. It was the first time that I had said words that I couldn't take back with an apology.

"SHUT UP WITH ALL THAT SCREAMING!"

Those were the last words I spoke to her and that's something I have to live the rest of my life with.

It's crazy when someone you love so dearly is gone forever.

Forever.

For ever.

KEEP LIVING.

There were so many firsts for me during this experience of grief. I witnessed my father, the strongest man I know, cry as if he was a kid again. I witnessed my mother, a woman who always had all the answers to any question I could ever ask, fail to form a coherent thought.

Now, here we are, nine years later and the process continues. One day life is going great. You are filled with gratitude and joy, and you seem to forget the deep wound that lies within. And then suddenly without warning, there are the days when it feels like it was only yesterday. On those days you wonder how you managed to live this long without this person.

Are you living and loving with gratitude? I have learned through this experience to appreciate everyone God gave me before it's too late. Life is short but it can feel like long, never-ending torture when you lose someone who you never appreciated when they were alive. The memories of their time with you constantly replay in your mind like a never-ending loop, and you hope to somehow find a reset button so you can change things.

But life goes on and you have to just keep living.

I FEEL REGRET.

PRESSURE & EXPECTATIONS

*Feeling obligated to do something
Because of someone's expectations of you.*

*Everything you wish you'd done has now faded,
Yet that obsession of their wants is still in you.*

*I hear pressure makes diamonds, I ask why do you
limit me to a diamond.*

*I don't think there are any limitations
to the places I can go. Nonetheless like a diamond my
levity will last long.*

*This stress created by the words
Pressure & Expectations.*

*They feed my eagerness for a distraction,
But it's only temporary.*

*If only I had someone to help me process my stress
then maybe I'd be alright.*

- I Just Need To Sit & Process

I feel pressured to be the absolute best at everything I do. If I am not, I feel like a failure to everyone who believes in me.

THESE OVERWHELMING THOUGHTS CONTROLLED ME SO MUCH, THAT I STARTED TO HAVE PANIC ATTACKS. IF I COULD EXPLAIN DEATH IN ANY WAY, THAT WOULD BE IT.

I forgot how to breathe. My palms were sweaty. I was lightheaded to the point where my thoughts grew fuzzy. My heart felt like it was going to beat out my chest. In the midst of that turmoil, I remember asking myself, *"how did I get to this point?"*

"I'm disappointed."

Hearing those words from someone who you desire to please, such as a parent, partner or coach, can hurt worse than a broken bone. People can expect so many things out of you. Sometimes even things that they never communicated! As if you are an omniscient mind reader.

I'VE COME TO A CONCLUSION THAT THE ONLY PERSON'S EXPECTATIONS THAT MATTER IS THE PERSON WHO I SEE IN THE MIRROR.

SCREAMING AT THE MAN IN THE MIRROR.

THERE'S A PLACE WE GO THAT NO ONE ELSE KNOWS, WHERE MYSTERIES ABOUND & DARKNESS GROWS.

For me, that place is in my bathroom, when I stand over the sink to wash my hands, and catch a glimpse of my reflection. In that moment, all the thoughts and emotions that I had avoided throughout the day rush to the forefront of my mind.

When will the insecurities end?

Are my dreams too big?

Am I setting a good example for anyone to follow?

Do I make my family proud? Will I ever find love?

I get caught up in contemplation of the pointlessness of life, the futility and frustration of the same things over, and over, and over again.

After all the struggles that I have faced and the sacrifices I've made to get where I am today, I'm still fighting, asking life, *"I have given all I have to you, but what do I get in return?"*

I know someday I'll have to wake up, and go back to it — the real world. Until then I'll close my eyes, make a wish and sleep.

I FEEL LOST.

FEAR OF SELF-LOVE

You look in the mirror and don't like what you see.

*The feeling of your life not being
enough for your liking.*

'Self-love is the best love' is something people say a lot.

While you constantly contemplate the what ifs.

What if I had their eyes...

What if I had their skin tone...

And even what if I had the life they had...

*The fear of not being accepted is taking over
My life like a food craving.*

-WHAT IF

Have you ever thought that you aren't good enough? I have always thought that me being my true self would only make others uncomfortable. I constantly changed and camouflaged myself to satisfy others. I often conceptualized their definition of *cool* and tried to duplicate it. But, how can you love someone else's life and not your own?

"Nobody can show you how to love yourself." I heard that in a song once. It injected an understanding in me that there is something about you someone will always have a problem with.

I have a painting in my bathroom that says "***SELF LOVE ANCHORS THE SOUL.***" It has taken me a while to find my own interpretation of it. To me, it means looking at yourself and being secure with what you see, not just on the outside but deep down in your soul.

It means self-love regardless of what any other person thinks, because you have found serenity in yourself. It speaks of a place that not even the most insecure and judgmental person can take you out of. Self-love is spreading that feeling you have for yourself out to everyone because you want people to feel as great as you do. More self-love would change the world.

I FEEL SELFISH, BUT FOR THE RIGHT REASONS.

PEACE BEFORE PURPOSE

We spend our whole life chasing something.

Eager to find our purpose in life.

Dreaming of that one opportunity.

But when we reach it, we don't get the same feeling
We had when we'd imagined it.

It's not good enough for us, we want more.

Looking for that sense of wholeness, because
We want to feel that feeling we had in our mind

- FULFILLMENT

I did that a lot — complained about the things I didn't have and where I was in my life.

I USED TO DO THAT A LOT, INSTEAD OF FOCUSING ON HOW BLESSED I AM AND HOW MUCH WORSE THINGS COULD BE.

I had to have a conversation with myself one day and it ended with me having a moment of enlightenment. I looked at the chair and thought to myself,

"This chair's sole purpose in life is to be sat in every day. Different people sit in it daily. They even leave dents in it and mess it up. Yet the chair does nothing but continues to fulfills its purpose in this world."

We look at the chair and find it mundane and pointless but the chair is serving its purpose!

COULD IT BE THAT I LACKED PURPOSE?

Because I definitely wasn't at peace with who I was and that day I was determined to make a change. In that moment I thought about my life, and the reasons why I felt unclear about my purpose in life.

HOW I FOUND PEACE.

I know someone who has experienced ultimate peace and have found their true purpose in life. This person is my aunt, Keisha Chambers, certified life coach.

"Peace is a very indescribable thing," she says. *"It's experienced in numerous ways."*

As for me, I found peace in my life by finally understanding that worrying and living life in fear don't solve anything. I feel like my soul is smiling now. All the pain I've faced bravely and even hesitantly, is now on my side and doesn't battle against me. Instead, the pain fuels and propels me forward.

PART II.

BEFORE THE PAIN

THE MAN I AM TODAY.

All these experiences that I have had, and the battles that I have faced have made me a better man. There are still and will always be more battles of course, but I'm better able to overcome them because of my new-found strength. I don't mean to imply that I've mastered handling my mental issues — not at all. But I am no longer struggling with mental health. Instead, I now know how to take regular steps to make daily improvements to my mental health.

I've found certain people who will listen to me without judgement. This social support has proven to be a blessing and a gift. In opening up myself and being transparent and real with others, I have released myself from the burden of chasing the elusive target of perfection. I accept me — with all my hang-ups and issues — and have found persons who accept me as well.

As for personal coping strategies: I pray and journal daily, and engage in group bible study regularly. Prayer and journaling have both helped me to accept my lack of control with some things, while helping me to think more clearly about the things that I can control.

I have made a habit to write down how I feel and I'm better because of it. Journaling has proven therapeutic for me and also helps me to get clarity and regain balance. It provides me with an outlet to introspect, release stress and ease feelings of distress. Group Bible study is how I share and deepen my faith with others.

As an athletic man, I enjoy the release of working out, running and playing basketball. The pandemic and these record-breaking low temperatures in Dallas have limited my opportunities to engage in these activities. Nonetheless, I try to do what I can in-doors, or outdoors when the circumstances permit.

This journey has not been without growth as I have learned various lessons through my pain experience.

I know that there is purpose in my pain.

I know that my pain was necessary for the destiny that God has for me.

I know that I am not weak for being expressive or being open about my mental health challenges. I am bold.

I am not a victim — I am a victor.

I HAVE NOT REACHED THE PEAK OF WHAT GOD HAS FOR ME JUST YET.

MENTAL FREEDOM.

The war is over.

I have found peace within this battle of pain. The pains of identity crisis, love, loss and insecurity are now gone.

Peace: it's this amazing feeling that I can't adequately explain. You will only understand it when you experience it. I don't know if I've found my true purpose yet but I am enjoying the journey of self-discovery.

Finally, I am at peace.

NOTE OF THANKS.

Damn, it's kinda crazy that I wrote this. This has been a wild ride.

Thank you for sticking with me through this book. Thank you for taking off your shoes and taking a walk in mine.

I can say honestly that it was not easy exposing the most painful parts of my journey to you but I am glad I did. If it made you gain perspective through your own pain experience, crack a smile, gave you a laugh, learn something new or just kept you from sitting in the dark depths of your mind, then I believe it was worth it.

If you're a black man, I hope I helped you feel bolder and more comfortable to express your truth even if that truth includes mental health issues.

Now go on and make your pain count! Find some positive in your pain.

Want to connect? I would love to hear from you.

Email **upnextprospects@gmail.com**
Instagram **@leftyymike_**

BE BLESSED & STAY SAFE,
MICHAEL

www.ingramcontent.com/pod-product-compliance
Lightning Source LLC
Chambersburg PA
CBHW060704280326
41933CB00012B/2291